THE LEARNING WORKS SCIENCE SERIES

FISHES

Written and Illustrated by Beverly Armstrong

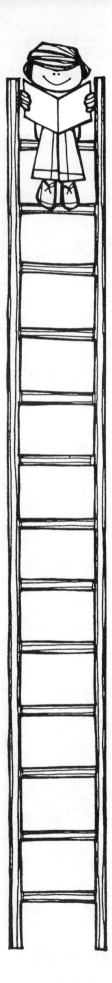

The
Learning
Works

Edited by Sherri M. Butterfield

Contents

FISHES © 1988—The Learning Works, Inc.

Amazon Leaf Fish

Hanging almost motionless in the waters of South American ponds and streams, this two-inch-long fish resembles a dead leaf. A dark line hides its eye, and the male even has a "stem" protruding from his chin. The leaf fish drifts slowly toward its prey—a water insect or a small fish—and then suddenly shoots out its strange extensible mouth to enclose and gobble its meal. These fish eat their weight in food each day and can swallow animals that are three-fourths of their own length.

There are eight species of leaf fish. Four are found in Asia, one in West Africa, and three in the Amazon basin.

Coloring Clues

The leaf fish may be mottled brown, golden yellow, or dull green.

Activity Safari

1. A leaf fish can eat a thousand inch-long fish in a year. How many feet are in a thousand inches?

2. The adjectives listed below may all be used to describe the leaf fish. Do you know the meanings of all five of them? If not, find their definitions in a dictionary.

   camouflaged   carnivorous
   cannibalistic   mottled
                     voracious

3. Another animal that looks like part of a plant is the giant stick insect. Its body is thirteen inches long! To draw a life-sized picture of this animal, enlarge the pattern shown below onto a six-by-twenty-inch piece of paper.

   Enlarge this drawing so that each square measures two inches by two inches.

Amazon Leaf Fish (*Monocirrhus polyacanthus*)

Atlantic Flying Gurnard

Flying gurnards are found in the warm waters of the Atlantic and Indian oceans. The Atlantic flying gurnard is one foot long. It has huge pectoral fins that can be snapped open to startle predators or used as wings in short glides above the water's surface. Flying gurnards can also swim or use their thin, leglike pelvic fins to walk along the sea floor. These fish feed on prawns and other small crustaceans. Despite their small size, Atlantic flying gurnards are aggressive and will even attempt to defend their territories against skin divers by marching forward, spreading their pectoral fins, and grunting fiercely.

Coloring Clues

The Atlantic flying gurnard has a tan body with brown, white, and light blue spots. Its pectoral fins are tan and white with bright blue-green stripes and spots.

Activity Safari

1. **Dactylopterus,** the name for this genus of fish, comes from the Greek words **daktylos,** meaning "finger," and **pteron,** meaning "wing." Does this name provide an accurate description of the flying gurnard? What is a **pterodactyl**?

2. Do some research to learn about one or more of the flying and gliding animals listed below.

flying dragon (draco)	a lizard whose ribs form wide "wings"
flying fish	glides above the water on winglike fins
flying fox	a fruit-eating bat with a five-foot wingspan
flying phalanger	a furry marsupial from Australia
flying snake	the paradise tree snake, which glides between branches
flying squirrel	found in North America, Europe, and Asia

Altantic Flying Gurnard (*Dactylopterus volitans*)

Blue Marlin

The blue marlin may be fifteen feet long and weigh half a ton. This fish can fold its fins into grooves along the sides of its body. Streamlined in this way, it shoots forward with each thrust of its powerful tail and may reach a speed of fifty miles per hour. There have been instances in which a marlin, traveling at high speed, has accidentally run into a ship, and its pointed beak has penetrated more than a foot of solid wood.

The marlin is a hungry hunter. It pursues schools of fish for days at a time, striking out with its pointed beak and then eating the fish it has killed. The only enemies of the blue marlin are large sharks and people, and a shark can catch a marlin only when the marlin is tired, sick, or injured.

Coloring Clues

The body of this marlin is blue above and silvery white below. Its dorsal fin is bright blue.

Activity Safari

1. The **narwhal,** a marine mammal, has a single straight tusk resembling the marlin's beak. The **sawfish** also has a long, strange snout. Do some research to find out more about these animals.

2. A 1500-pound marlin can eat a 150-pound fish. If you ate something one-tenth of your weight, how much would it weigh?

3. Make a bar graph on which you compare the lengths of the blue marlin with the lengths of the other fishes listed below. These lengths are given in feet.

alligator gar	5	great barracuda	9
Atlantic sturgeon	10	hammerhead shark	12
blue marlin	15	muskellunge	6
conger eel	7	yellowfin tuna	9

FISHES © 1988—The Learning Works, Inc.

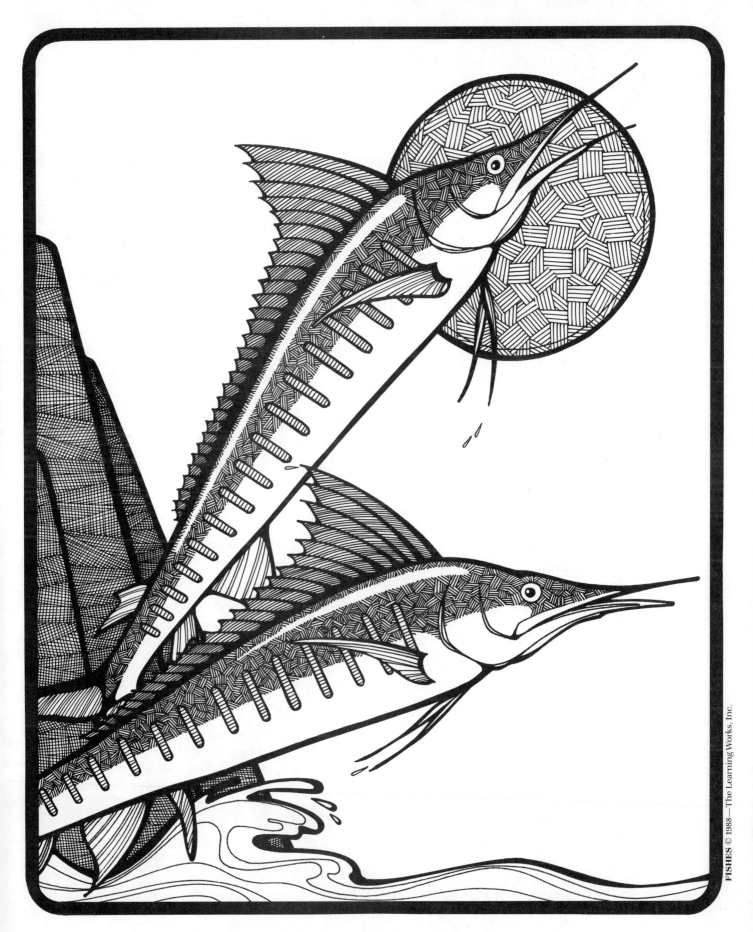

Blue Marlin (*Makaira nigricans*)

Blue Ribbon Eel

The blue ribbon eel belongs to the family of moray eels. It is thirty inches long; other species in this family may be up to ten feet long. By day, these tropical fish hide among rocks or in coral beds. At night, they emerge as snakelike predators, feeding on any animals that can be swallowed whole. Morays have a reputation for viciousness, but are generally shy around people and will attack only if threatened. A skin diver's hand reaching into a moray's hole may look like a delicious baby octopus! Morays almost always have their mouths open; to live, they must pump a continuous flow of water through their gills.

Coloring Clues

The blue ribbon eel is bright blue with a gold face and yellow eyes. Its dorsal fin is yellow with a white edge and a fine red line. The short tube through which water leaves the gills is yellow.

Activity Safari

1. Morays have a good sense of smell, which helps them detect both predators and prey. Which scents warn *you* of danger? Which foods do you especially like to smell? What aromas do you detect at home, at school, or in a park or shopping center?

2. Morays are sometimes known as painted eels. Many are marked with colorful stripes and spots. Draw a long moray eel and decorate it, using pens, paints, or crayons. Think of a descriptive name for your eel.

3. You may have heard the expression "as slippery as an eel." Can you think of animals to match the adjectives listed below?

   as **friendly** as _____

   as **graceful** as _____

   as **huge** as _____

   as **quick** as _____

   as **silent** as _____

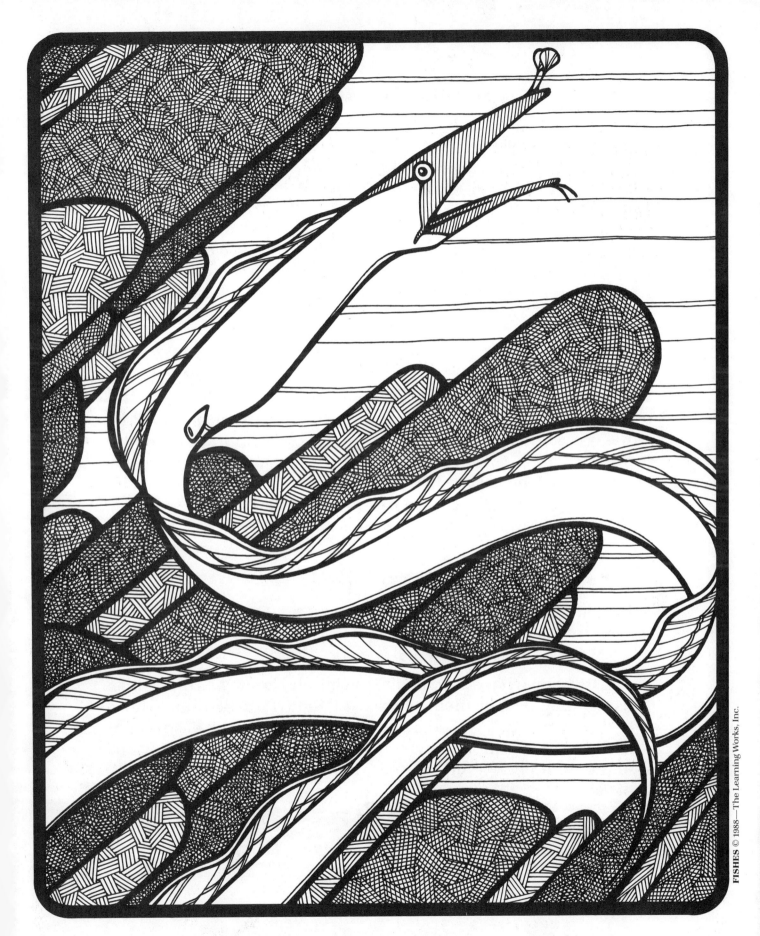

Blue Ribbon Eel (*Muraena quaesita*)

Clown Triggerfish

This gaudy tropical fish may be up to twenty inches long. It glides among coral reefs in search of crabs, sea urchins, and shellfish, which it grinds up with its strong, sharp teeth. Triggerfish are aggressive and solitary. When frightened, first they dive into holes and cracks among the rocks and coral. Then they erect the long, strong spines of their dorsal fins, wedging themselves in so that predators cannot remove them. These dorsal spines, for which the triggerfish is named, may also be used as weapons. There are thirty species of triggerfish.

Coloring Clues

The clown triggerfish has a black body with colorful markings. Its mouth is orange, and there is an orange line around it. A yellow stripe crosses the fish's face. Its eyes are brown. On the back of the fish is a yellow area with blue spots. The large spots below are light blue or white. The tail is yellow and black; there is a yellow spot at its base. The two largest fins are mostly blue but have orange stripes at their bases, along the body.

Activity Safari

1. Imagine that you work at a public aquarium which is adding a large exhibit of tropical marine fishes. Design a poster or bumper sticker to promote this exhibit.

2. The triggerfish has a rigid body; it swims by rippling its fins. Other fishes may propel themselves with their tails or their whole bodies. Some glide gracefully through the water, some dash wildly about, and some move slowly and cautiously. At a public aquarium or pet store, observe and compare the movements of several kinds of fishes.

Clown Triggerfish (*Balistes conspicillum*)

Dwarf Seahorse

Gliding gracefully among the turtle grass and floating seaweed in shallow bays of the Gulf of Mexico, these tiny seahorses look more like miniature dragons than fish. They suck up tiny crustaceans with their pointed snouts and curl their prehensile tails around plants to avoid being swept out to sea. The male has a special pouch in which the female lays her eggs. The young develop inside this pouch for eight to ten days, nurtured by food and oxygen from their father's bloodstream. At "birth," they are popped out into the ocean by contractions of the father's body. The babies are minute replicas of their parents.

Coloring Clues

Dwarf seahorses are found in shades of brown, orange, and yellow. When frightened, they turn dark brown or black.

Activity Safari

1. This tiny seahorse grows to be only $1\frac{5}{8}$ inches long. On a piece of paper, draw a line of this length and label it "dwarf seahorse." Then draw and label lines representing the lengths of the animals listed below. These lengths are given in inches.

bee hummingbird	$2\frac{1}{4}$	pygmy shrew	$2\frac{1}{2}$
least tree frog	$\frac{5}{8}$	striped newt	2
newborn kangaroo	1	thread snake	$4\frac{3}{4}$

2. When a seahorse is moving quickly, its dorsal fin ripples thirty-five times every second. How many times does it ripple in a minute?

3. In each pair of animals listed below, one carries its young in a pouch and the other does not. Which is which? If you don't know, refer to an encyclopedia or a book about mammals.

armadillo kangaroo	koala hedgehog	raccoon opossum	weasel wombat

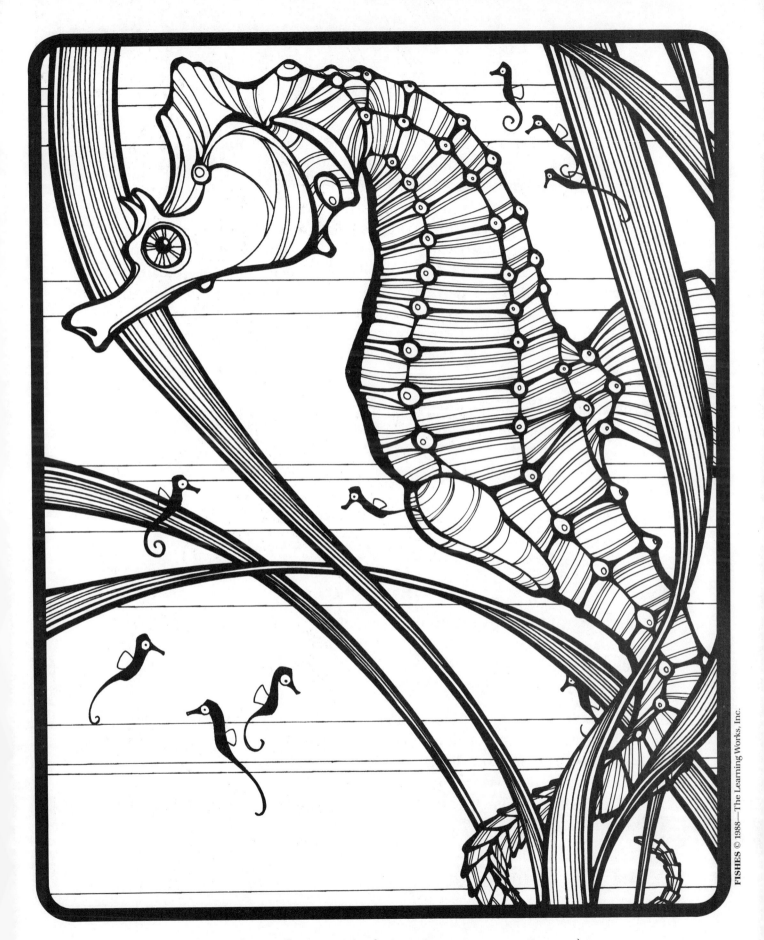

Dwarf Seahorse (*Hippocampus zosterae*)

Eyed Electric Ray

A strangely shaped fish, the eyed electric ray is a poor swimmer and spends most of its time partly buried in the sand of shallow marine waters. Its gill openings and protruding eyes are on the upper surface of its flattened body. Its mouth, on the underside, siphons up the small crustaceans on which it feeds. The eyed electric ray's shock-producing organs are located on its "shoulders" and represent one-sixth of its total body weight. Triggered by messages from the ray's brain, these organs can produce a shock stronger than that generated by a household current. Though occasionally used to stun fish for food, this shock is more often used as a defense mechanism. After discharging, the ray must rest for a while to "recharge" itself.

This species of electric ray lives in the Atlantic Ocean and is two feet long. Other electric rays are up to five feet in length.

Coloring Clues

The eyed electric ray is sandy brownish yellow with round blue spots, or "eyes."

Activity Safari

1. In ancient Greece and Rome, physicians used electric rays to treat a variety of ailments. The treatment consisted of pressing a live ray against the patient's feet or forehead. Design an advertisement for this primitive "shock treatment."

2. The scientific name for the eyed electric ray is ***Torpedo torpedo.*** This name comes from the Latin verb *torpere,* which means "to be sluggish or numb." The **torpedo,** an underwater missile fired from warships, was named for this fish. On a separate sheet of paper, list at least five motor vehicles that have been named for animals.

Eyed Electric Ray (*Torpedo torpedo*)

Koi

The ancestors of today's koi were dull-colored carp, which were probably raised in Iran for food. A thousand years ago, traders carried these fish to Europe and Asia. In Japan, the orange or reddish offspring that the carp sometimes produced were saved and bred. Eventually, many dazzling colors and patterns were created.

Though koi look like goldfish, they are a different species. Koi may grow to be more than two feet long, while goldfish rarely exceed eight to twelve inches in length. Also, koi have a pair of whiskerlike barbels, which goldfish lack.

Many people collect koi and keep them as pets. To meet this demand, thousands of koi have been exported from Japan in the past forty years. Koi learn to recognize their owners and come to take food from their hands. Collectors keep them in outdoor ponds, sometimes bringing their fish together for shows and competitions. A good koi may be worth several hundred dollars.

Coloring Clues

Koi are marked with red, orange, yellow, blue, black, and/or white.

Activity Safari

1. Koi may live for sixty years. If a koi hatched today and lived sixty years, in what year would it die?

2. You can teach a goldfish to read! To do so, you will need a goldfish in a glass container, goldfish food, and a three-by-five-inch piece of paper. Print the words **Go to the top** on the paper. Each time you feed your fish (two or three times a day), first hold the paper near the container so that the fish can see it. Then feed the fish. Soon your fish will learn that seeing the paper means food is coming, and it will go to the surface to eat each time it sees the paper. Your fish cannot really read; but it has been conditioned to respond when it sees the paper, and will continue to do so even if it is *not* fed every time.

Koi (*Cyprinus carpio*)

Lionfish

The lionfish lives among coral reefs in warm marine waters. Spreading its array of fins and spines, this twelve-inch creature moves through the water like a ship under full sail. Its pectoral fins, located behind the gills, are each longer than its body. Lionfish can move forward fearlessly because many of their spines carry venom and can inflict very painful, possibly deadly wounds. These spines are used only for defense, not for killing prey. To eat, the lionfish simply snaps up smaller fish and crustaceans with its huge mouth.

The lionfish belongs to the scorpionfish family, which includes more than three hundred species. One of these is the squat, lumpy stonefish. The sharp spines on the stonefish's back are connected to huge venom glands and cause agonizing injury to anyone who has the misfortune of stepping on them.

Coloring Clues

The lionfish is striped with red-orange and white bands.

Activity Safari

1. The lionfish is found in the Indian Ocean and the Red Sea. Find these two bodies of water on a world map.

2. Lionfish are sometimes sold in pet stores. Do you think that people should be allowed to keep such deadly animals as pets? Why or why not? Should they be required to keep the fish in a covered, locked aquarium and to post a warning sign?

3. Because of the lionfish's unusual appearance and its ability to poison would-be tormentors, it is also known as the cobrafish, the dragonfish, the firefish, the stingfish, the turkeyfish, the waspfish, and the zebrafish. Can you make up alternate, similarly descriptive names for the animals listed below?

   dalmatian (dog)   grasshopper   penguin
   giraffe   guinea pig   raccoon

Lionfish (*Pterois volitans*)

Mudskipper

The mudskipper is a funny looking, froglike fish that hops, skips, and flops across mud flats and mangrove swamps in Africa, Asia, and islands of the southwestern Pacific Ocean. Mudskippers come out of water to bask in the sun and to feed on insects and small crustaceans. Some of these fish can even climb trees! While on land, mudskippers carry water in spongy sacs in their gill chambers; they must return to the sea frequently to moisten their skins and to refill these built-in "canteens" with mouthfuls of water.

Some mudskippers dig vertical burrows in mud near the water's edge. These fish look like tiny, droll dragons as they defend their homes by waving their fins, rolling their eyes, and yawning at each other.

Coloring Clues

The mudskipper is tan with brown and blue-green spots. There are blue and white stripes on the two dorsal fins along its back.

Activity Safari

1. The mudskipper has eyes set high on its head. They enable the animal to see what is happening above the water's surface while the rest of its body is hidden below. What reptiles and amphibians have similarly placed eyes?

2. Mudskippers are amphibious animals. The English word **amphibious** comes from the Greek words **amphi** and **bio.** What do these two words mean? Where can an amphibious animal live? Where does an amphibious vehicle travel?

3. Imagine that your school has a water polo team called the Mudskippers. Design a T-shirt, tote bag, or other item for the team. Use the drawing below or create your own.

Mudskipper (*Periophthalmus koelreuteri*)

Northern Pike

Lurking motionless among a lake's plants and shadows, this great predator watches for passing fishes, frogs, and water birds. Sighting a victim, it shoots forward with a thrust of its powerful tail. Quick as a flash, the pike grabs its helpless prey in its gaping, sharp-toothed mouth and swallows the animal whole. The fish may rest for a week after a large meal.

The northern pike is found in freshwater lakes and streams from the Great Lakes to Alaska. It also lives in Europe. This fish may be four and one-half feet long and weigh nearly fifty pounds. The females are generally larger than the males.

Coloring Clues

The northern pike's upper body is dull green with yellow spots. Its underside is light yellow or white. Its eyes and fins are deep golden yellow.

Activity Safari

1. An adult pike has few enemies other than people. Which of the animals listed below have few enemies and which are preyed upon by several kinds of animals?

duck	lion
eagle	rabbit
frog	wolf

2. The pike is named after a weapon that was used in medieval times. In a dictionary or an encyclopedia, find a description of the weapon known as a **pike**, or **pikestaff**.

3. The northern pike is related to the muskellunge, which shares part of its North American habitat. Which of these two fishes is usually larger? In what ways are the two species similar? In what ways are they different? Look for information in an encyclopedia or a book about fishes.

Northern Pike (*Esox lucius*)

Powder Blue Surgeonfish

The surgeonfish carries a switchblade! Near the base of its tail is a pair of razor-sharp spines. Usually, they are folded down into grooves; but if the fish is alarmed or angry, they snap open, becoming effective weapons as the surgeonfish thrashes its tail from side to side. When not defending themselves, surgeonfish are peaceful plant-eaters. They move about in schools, nibbling algae from coral beds with their finely pointed mouths.

There are more than two hundred species of surgeonfish, which are also known as lancetfish, doctorfish, and barbers. They are widespread in warmer areas of the Indian and Pacific oceans. Most of them are brightly colored.

Coloring Clues

The powder blue surgeonfish has a bright blue-green body. Its eyes are red. A white-bordered mask covers its face, and there are white markings near its mouth. Its dorsal (back) fin is yellow with a blue border. There is a yellow area at the base of its tail. Its pelvic and anal fins (located below the body) are white; its tail is white with a black border.

Activity Safari

1. Surgeonfish swim slowly. Because they eat algae, they do not need to go fast to catch their food. Because they are protected by spines, they rarely need to flee from predators. Name three animals that do need to move quickly to catch their food, and three that must be able to escape from fast-moving predators.

2. The surgeonfish swims by moving its **pectoral fins.** Which ones are they? You have **pectoral muscles.** Where are they located?

3. Design a stamp bearing the message **Protect Marine Life.** In your design, include the value of the stamp and the name of the country issuing it.

FISHES © 1988—The Learning Works, Inc.

Powder Blue Surgeonfish (*Acanthurus leucosternon*)

Siamese Fighting Fish

Developed from a drab, short-finned wild fish, today's Siamese fighting fish is a dazzling jewel. A special chamber above its gills enables it to take oxygen from the air as well as from the water; therefore, it can survive in stagnant ponds and small containers. When breeding, the male blows a nest of sticky bubbles on the water's surface. Here he deposits and guards the female's eggs.

Female fighting fish are short-finned, somewhat drab, and peaceful. Male fighting fish are long-finned, colorful, and fiercely territorial. When one male sees another male fighting fish (or even his own reflection) within his territory, his color intensifies and he spreads his fins and tail as a signal to the interloper that he is *not* welcome. He may even attack, biting the other fish's body and tearing its flowing fins and tail to shreds.

Coloring Clues

The Siamese fighting fish may be bright red, blue, or green, or a combination of these colors. For example, it may have a blue body and red fins.

Activity Safari

1. The Siamese fighting fish is also known as a **betta,** and is sometimes kept in aquariums. Make a word search puzzle using some or all of the names of these aquarium fishes.

angelfish	cichlid	gourami	platy
barb	danio	guppy	rasbora
betta	discus	molly	swordtail
catfish	glassfish	panchax	tetra

2. Siamese fighting fish play an important part in controlling the spread of **malaria.** Read about this disease in an encyclopedia. What are its symptoms? How does it affect people? How is it spread? In what ways might these fish help to control it?

Siamese Fighting Fish (*Betta splendens*)

Viperfish

The ocean's dark depths are home to a host of eerie creatures. There are goggle-eyed fishes with gaping jaws. Some have huge teeth; others have none. Some have threadlike fins or feelers that are longer than their bodies; others' fins are small, stubby paddles. Most of these deep-sea fishes have luminous spots or light-emitting organs which enable them to locate each other—and their prey—in the inky darkness.

The viperfish jiggles a light-emitting organ at the end of its long, thin dorsal fin to attract other fishes. Then it grabs and gobbles them with its needle-like teeth. Its stomach can stretch to hold a huge meal. No plants—and few animals—can survive in the depths where viperfish live, and food must be snatched whenever it is available.

Coloring Clues

The viperfish is silvery blue or gray. The light-emitting organs along its lower body are yellow. The light-emitting organs near its eye are red.

Activity Safari

1. The light-emitting organs on a viperfish are also called **photophores.** What is the meaning of the combining form **photo,** which is a part of this longer word? If you do not know, find it in a dictionary.

2. Viperfish are often found more than a mile below the water's surface. To get an idea of how deep this is, locate two points in your town or city that are one mile apart.

3. The deep sea where viperfish live is very cold and very dark. What do you think it would be like to live in darkness for a month, with just a flashlight to guide you? Name ten activities, sensations, or sights that you would miss.

Viperfish (*Chauliodis sloani*)

Fish Facts

The coelacanth is a very primitive fish. It was believed to have been extinct for sixty million years, but in 1938 a living specimen was caught near South Africa.

The blind cave fish, living in dark underground pools, has no eyes. It navigates by feeling water pressure and vibrations.

African lungfishes can survive being buried in dried out mud for as long as four years.

The upside-down catfish swims in an inverted position.

Some species of goby are only one-half inch long when fully grown.

The electric eel can discharge 550 volts.

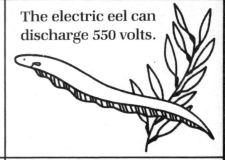

The largest of all fishes is the whale shark. It may be over fifty feet long and weigh more than forty thousand pounds.

The stonefish is the most venomous of all fishes.

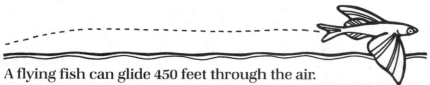

A flying fish can glide 450 feet through the air.

The strange ocean sunfish, or headfish, may be ten feet long and weigh two tons.

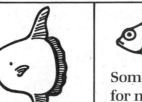

Some goldfish live for more than forty years.

Salmon hatch in freshwater streams, then live in the ocean for four or five years. When ready to spawn, they travel as many as three thousand miles, returning to their original hatching sites.